The 13th Sunday after Pentecost

The 13th Sunday after Pentecost

poems

Joseph Bathanti

LOUISIANA

STATE

UNIVERSITY

PRESS

Baton Rouge

Published by Louisiana State University Press
Copyright © 2016 by Joseph Bathanti
All rights reserved
Manufactured in the United States of America
LSU Press Paperback Original
First printing

DESIGNER: *Mandy McDonald Scallan*
TYPEFACE: *Calluna*
PRINTER AND BINDER: *LSI*

Library of Congress Cataloging-in-Publication Data
Names: Bathanti, Joseph, author.
Title: The 13th Sunday after Pentecost : poems /
Joseph Bathanti.
Other titles: Thirteenth Sunday after Pentecost
Description: Baton Rouge : Louisiana State University
Press, 2017. | "LSU
   Press paperback original."
Identifiers: LCCN 2016012829| ISBN 978-0-8071-
6461-7 (paper : alk. paper) | ISBN
   978-0-8071-6462-4 (pdf) | ISBN 978-0-8071-6463-1
(epub) | ISBN 978-0-8071-6464-8 (mobi)
Classification: LCC PS3602.A89 A6 2017 | DDC
811/.6—dc23
LC record available at https://lccn.loc.gov/2016012829

For Joan Ever

Contents

I. OMEGA STREET

Baseball 3
Affliction 5
Betsy Wetsy 7
Angel Food 8
The Huckster 10
Pass Over My Life in Silence 12
Sleepwalking in Purgatory 13
DiDomeni 14

II. CONFITEOR

Goldfinger 23
The DeNinno Sisters 25
High Mass 27
Holy God 29
The Cold War 31
The 13th Sunday after Pentecost 35
Sister Thomasine 38
Good Friday: March 24, 1967 39
Emerson Street 41
Brooks Brothers Shirts 43
The Pittsburgh Athletic Association 46
Connecticut 48
Stag 50
The North Game 52
The Lobotomy Running Schenley Oval 54
Migraine 55

III. GENITORI

Angels 59

The Little Noise 60

My Mother and Father Falling 62

Joe and Rose 63

Haircut 64

My Father at the Montréal Musée des Beaux-Arts 67

Bracciole 69

The Hour of the Wolf 70

The First Sunday of Advent 71

Burying Saint Joseph 73

Labriola's 75

Acknowledgments 77

I. OMEGA STREET

I am Alpha and Omega, the first and the last: . . . What thou seest, write in a book . . .

—REVELATIONS I:II

Baseball

I learned to play baseball on Omega Street,
in the lot across from DiDomeni Row.
The Left field line was Chippanellis' grape vine.
Right was bound by a barbed-wire compound
of rusted I-beams and railroad ties
oozing creosote and tetanus.

Straightaway, deep in Center, quaked
the threshold of Saints Peter and Paul—
its steeples higher than the roof at Forbes Field,
over which Babe Ruth launched his last homer.
On the convent lawn,
the American flag clapped its pole.

We patched together teams of pick up:
the Negro brothers, Anthony and Raymond Jefferson;
the DiDomeni girl who became a nun;
straggled gypsy children, from the projects,
just off the boat, who spoke no English.

Out of that parched yellow earth, cracked and scribed,
grew igneous, sharp metallic rock
(tiny purple meteorites),
dandelions, chickweed, broken glass,
panels of turquoise tile we unearthed
from the foundry berm for bases.
Hitting a taped ball with a taped bat,
running everything out, as I'd been taught,
my sins, beneath the summer sun,
seared from my soul.
My flat, homely glove whispered
the secret of catching.

The field was a cut-through to Mass.
You had to cross one-way Reiter Street,
where Pasquale Bellasario,
turned berserk by *West Side Story,*
lurked with his BB pistol.
He was more than just a bad boy;
Lucifer had punched a needle in his arm.

When I dashed for the plate,
he shot at me.
But I was at peace, invulnerable.
I had wrested from Jesus His promise
of eternal life—so happy,
so fleet, nothing could snare me.

Affliction

The summer baseball seduced me,
I'd begun to notice affliction.
Tadzio, the handsome Polish man
Mrs. Scott rented to—his last name
a string of grinding consonants—
had on the underside of his throwing arm
a supernumerary nipple.
Like everyone on Omega Street,
he had suffered in the World War.
We called him *Teddy.* Younger,
less aged than our fathers,
he didn't rise and leave in the smoky dawn
for the mill or brick yard.

My mother held his good looks against him.
They could only be a ruse, a cover-up.
Polack. At least he was clean.
He wore white shirts to play baseball with us
in the lot across from DiDomeni's.
He taught me to overwinter
my little Wilson glove,
dose it with neatsfoot and lanolin,
truss it in twine, a ball in its pocket,
remand it to the dark cellar shelf,
and resist the temptation to unbind it
until The Feast of Saint Joseph.

I had nightmares about his glove,
a first baseman's mitt,
Venus flytrap pink, freakish
as a crab claw;
its pretty flange, rawhide-
stitched, medieval web sticky
enough to snag a rodent.
He let us put our hands in it.

On a whim, or if we begged,
he hit us flies with his massive
38 ounce *Louisville Slugger,*
archaic script in the ellipsoid brand,
Hank Greenberg burnt into the barrel.
With one cut, he lifted the ball higher
than the steeples of Saints Peter and Paul.

Betsy Wetsy

Apprenticed to motherhood,
Marie made pot holders on a wee loom
and gave Betsy Wetsy her teeny bottle
with real formula that disappeared
with each prurient suck
of her plastic mouth:
bright red, coquettish,
pursed like Betty Boop's,
the same black burlesque curls,
starlet lashes—
looks that spelled trouble,
etymology of the word *doll.*
One of her blue eyes was tetched.
It lolled open of its own volition.
Marie loved her all the more for it.
Betsy Wetsy could wet,
her singular feat,
her *raison d'être,*
what we all waited for.
Scandalous: a hole
out of which pee dribbled,
soaking her dotted swiss.
Marie bathed, then diapered, her.
I despised her undressed.
Mother washed her clothes with ours.
My father built her a cradle.
I thought she was one of us—
that eye fixed on me.

Angel Food

Saturday, when my father worked turns
at the mill—4 to 12,
double-time-and-a-half—
my mother baked a cake.
From the whisk and spatula,
Marie and I licked batter,
then floured the greased pans.

We were forbidden to slam doors,
jump from the landing,
even raise our voices;
the cake would fall.
At that concussive instant
(carelessness, an accident),
the baking powder—secreting
vapors urging the cake to rise—
is at its most volatile,
the crucible housing oxygen
fragile, about to detonate.

Complicit in the mystery
behind the oven door,
we tiptoed solemnly
winter's sacramental hush.
Yet the temptation to lift
then slam a sash obsessed me.
Were the cake to fall
it was ours immediately,
unceremoniously, in un-iced fragments
with our hands from a common plate:
orange angel food
my mother tried on a lark.
A failed cake made her so blue,
as if she'd brought it upon herself—
and not my desire.
I prayed the cake fall.

Elbow on the table, a hand
worried into her long brown hair,
she sat with Marie and me
in the dining room on Prince Street
and stared at us.
She never tasted the cake,
but smiled as we ate it—
as much as we wanted
even though we hadn't had supper.

The Huckster

The women on Prince and Omega streets
flocked to DiDomeni's Field
when *Cesare,* Caesar, the gypsy huckster,
arrived in his bright red pickup
spilling gorgeous produce,
flats of begonias and marigolds,
Cymbidium orchids, lemon ice,
elderberries, occasional magnums
of Florentine champagne,
and, in its season, dressed hare.

He looked like Paladin, Caravaggio,
what I, hanging on a fender,
stealing green grapes, recognized
as a cruel face, filthy with stubble,
rakish silent-movie mustache,
his every move exquisitely choreographed,
as if a wizard, spinning, out of thin air,
apricots, nectarines, peaches
with the complexion of Irish girls—
though dressed like an Abruzzi peasant,
white kerchief tied at his neck,
gold crucifix on its chain, black fedora.
He'd knifed johns on Larimer Avenue
over cards and girls.

The women, in sleeveless summer dresses,
fountains of hair scarved at their crowns,
change purses—my mother too—hurried
to haggle over the final crop of cherries,
damson plums, piled dripping, bloody
in the pan of his scales, its needle
jouncing like a Geiger counter.
Once he had them in his sway, he revealed
his cache of dirt-cheap hot cigarettes,
transistor radios, record albums.

The silk stockings he withheld
until the last, as if he'd conjured them,
and they possessed the power to turn
our mothers into queens.
He'd open a package,
tear out a flimsy gauntlet,
rustle his fist through its mouth,
and sheath it up his rippling arm.
Through the transparent weave,
thick black hairs magically sprouted,
as if proving his powers,
especially over women,
that he could make anything happen:
bargains, unimaginable luxury,
transform a huckster's arm
into the carnal leg of a beast.

Pass Over My Life in Silence

Rooted in the middle of Omega Street,
my grandmother at the camera stares
without the least portent of fear.

She wears the matriarchal frock, tam
brooched with a mother-of-pearl diadem.
A sneer bows her left upper lip,

making of her countenance a dare
to silence the storyteller.
Behind her glooms Goodwin's four-bay

Depression garage and its story
of ravaged garrets. Her shadow,
from which her brood issued,

splays like a turned-away shade
on the asphalt, cracked,
as is the photograph, from the album torn,

its inscription sealed forever
on its back by the flayed black
crepe to which it was pasted:

Pass over my life in silence.
Omega Street opens.
Into her shadow,

Grandmother falls.
From the rent earth
her children claw.

Sleepwalking in Purgatory

The house on Omega Street
had nothing to mark it
for having whelped seven children
but their fictions—
love foreswearing love.
When finally freed by death
of that cursed shackle of blood,
their ghosts, conscripted to tarry
in its abandonment,
until it was knocked down,
could not depart.
There remained in the cellar,
beneath the rafter and its noose,
a locked steamer trunk
with the documents
from Provincia diCaserta.
In night's black wool,
the children jar and pry.
The earth turns, suspires.
At first light, the elliptic shog
of the wrecking ball
remands them back to fire.

DiDomeni

We called it DiDomeni Row
because every soul in that span
of three-story, blonde brick rowhouses
licking out of Omega Street—

glutted, obese, haunted
by the embittered
Napolitano ghosts
of the diaspora—

was a DiDomeni. *Of God.*
They owned the bakery
I tripped into dusky afternoons
with three nickels from my mother's change purse

and instructions to buy a loaf of *crippled*—
split heels, fissures, *brutto,*
but cheaper, good as what sold
for perfect. Bread was bread.

My dad paced the Union side of a Wildcat,
washing dishes at the Kennilworth,
gutting out the steel strike
at the Edgar Thomson Works.

My mother collected *Compensation.*
Perhaps *crippled* was an admission of something,
humility at the least—a fine virtue
I wouldn't have known a thing about.

My parents, our entire family,
felt the DiDomenis held themselves too high
for what they were.
I learned to despise those with more than me,

yet loved my daily errand to the bakery.
It smelled like the Lord God of Hosts.
Behind glassed rows of Italian pastry,
ravishing as stained glass,

Mrs. DiDomeni,
as if just emerged from her bath,
silk summer frock, often barefoot,
peeked over stacked loaves

spreading the counter down upon me.
"A loaf of crippled, please?"
She smiled and handed me the broken bread,
DiDomeni elegantly scrivened in red

across its white sleeve. Then my reward:
"What cookie, *Caro Giuseppe?*"
her Petrarchan accent leavened
with the lassitude of wealth.

I wanted to kiss her naked feet,
to live inside her. Sex and money
were the same. In slick tissue,
she handed me the delicate cookie

I always chose and ate ceremonially
on the way home:
first, the fluted white *corpus,*
then the spall of fudge that crowned it,

held on my tongue until it dissolved.
She was too beautiful for the other women
on the street not to loathe:
regal cheekbones, magnificent hair,

the powdered bodice of Sophia Loren,
lazy almond eyes, alabaster teeth,
all that money. They said
she was Grazziella's apprentice *strega,*

a witch, a gypsy.
She cast the *malocchio.*
They said she had to get married.
It was Francesco,

her sissy son, she carried.
Moorish Francesco—a real shame—
fat superior face,
black oiled hoodlum-curl

twisted coquettishly over an eye.
He was beautiful too.
We crucified him for it.
Even in winter he went shirtless.

He loved his big belly.
Francesco had a Negro father,
a long-distance teamster rarely home.
Perhaps a Spaniard. A Cuban.

Anything was better than black.
Puerto Rican was better;
they said that about Roberto Clemente—
that he wasn't black, but Puerto Rican—

though the color of sizzling asphalt.
Francesco's dad was light-skinned;
that was a good thing.
I'd forget about him,

then suddenly he'd lumber his flame-blue tractor
majestically over the curb,
like a wyvern come to roost,
into the junk lot across from DiDomeni Row—

where we played baseball—
and park beyond the first-base line
in burdock and beggar lice.
Bright license plates from every state

hung from it like scales.
Even after he killed the engine,
it hissed and shuddered and smoked.
In a black Pirates cap,

gold gothic *P* at its crest,
tall and thin, gray mustache,
he descended silver rungs from the cab,
a little fan on its dashboard.

None of the men on the Omega Street had mustaches.
He wore dungarees.
His glance fell upon us, too bitter
to be wistful, but not unfriendly.

He missed the game;
Francesco didn't play.
He loitered a moment
until an errant ball strayed his way,

genuflected like an infielder,
gathered it up, cocked like he'd fire.
He could have killed us—
we were small children—

but he seemed fearful of us.
He never said a word, nor did we.
He held the baseball a moment;
then, like an amnesiac, smelled it,

lobbed it back; crossed Omega
and entered the house,
in the center of the row,
where his queen awaited him.

We knew this man as Mr. DiDomeni—
though that couldn't have been his name—
the black Mr. DiDomeni.
He never crossed the bakery's threshold.

Some said there were two husbands.
But that wasn't true.
There was just this man.
Poor Francesco: Look at the lips,

they'd say, the wiry hair.
There was an intimacy to punching
his unctuous porcine body
like he was mine to take it out on,

the half-breed, the superior boy.
I made him cry.
Wasn't that proof of something?
The slumbering tractor hulked in the weeds;

and, one day, when we gathered
to choose sides,
it would be vanished.
We heard—the entire street heard

(and they hated her for this too)—
Mrs. DiDomeni in the house,
like a singular Greek chorus,
her myhthic weeping.

Pigeons lined her gutters.
Crows draped the telephone wires.
DiDomeni bread was never absent
from our table.

II. Confiteor

Confiteor Deo omnipotenti . . .
—FROM *THE CONFITEOR*

Goldfinger

My mother (Baby), and her sisters,
Jay and Dolly, were the first to see *Goldfinger*
when it came to the Sheridan Square in East Liberty.
They discussed it over coffee and cigarettes
at Aunt Jay's kitchen table on the same street,
Omega, where they'd grown up—
a family of nine, in four rooms.

Shiny carnal dresses, jewelry, high heels,
the hips, the walks, the purses—
the almighty cheek. Precise as Joan Crawford—
wavy diademed tresses. They could have been starlets.
Their eyes—Maybelline lashes, smoldering
with the last of their dreams—
lent them the gaze of Dyads
as they smiled theatrically through lipstick
and Prince Matchabelli.
They saw right through Bond: *fit to kill.*
Never would they have never fallen
for the line he fed women.
Q was an ass—they cared little for the British—
his contraptions a little too fantastic.
Pussy Galore was going too far,
but they laughed.
Moneypenny was more their cup of tea;
they exulted sarcasm.

That Auric Goldfinger murdered Jill Masterson,
painting her gold, naked, face-down, on that bed,
was why I was forbidden to see the movie.
The Legion of Decency condemned it.
Before Vietnam, *naked* was the vilest thing on earth.
My mother and her sisters held these characters
liable for the vengeful tariffs of love—
as they did with each other,
their brothers, mother, and father.
As if Bond, Q, Moneypenny, Jill,
Oddjob, Pussy, and Goldfinger
resided on Omega Street, possessed
of free will, stamped with Original Sin—
feckless as the rest of us.

Christmas morning, the 007 attaché case,
its catches booby-trapped with tear gas,
lay under our tree.
Inside, ingeniously disguised,
were a disassembled AR-7,
with infrared scope; throwing knife;
gold sovereigns; and a long black silencer
for Bond's Beretta 418
concealed in a tube of shaving soap.
Exact pressure, at secret points
on the case's handle, released
the cyanide suicide pill.

The DeNinno Sisters

A black-and-white studio portrait
documents my mother and her sisters
at the Christian Mothers banquet,
The Embers in East Liberty—
Feb. 18, 1947
stamped in purple on its back—
at a table frothed in white linen,
gardenia compotes, silver, china,
crystal, corsages, cigarettes
demurring in milk-glass ashtrays.

They could be waiting for the Eucharist,
waiting to be ravished, slaughtered
for the faith, yet my mother and aunts
have not indulged in the sacraments
since Matrimony. The only man permitted
is the handsome Jesuit Rector,
Father Beatrix, before him
a cruet of Inver House
and monogrammed Scripto
for his Luckies, red bull's-eye
on the package: Mary's Immaculate Heart.
The parish women are in love with him:
blinding Roman collar, spit and image
of Charles Boyer in *Gaslight*—
charming, urbane, Alsatian accent.

Father's bevy of nuns,
Sisters of Divine Providence,
a German order, also worship him.
Prussian habits, black as wire, they smile
from the prim bespectacled caves of their wimples.
My mother and aunts call them *beasts.*
Beatrix, the Christ-proxy, the *playboy,*
thinks he's the Christ.
They have his number too.
Only a fool would cross them
in their imperious pissed-off dresses.
They dare someone to mouth off.
But, immured at their stations
in this photograph, posed, beaming,
they'll neither flinch nor abandon
their perfect silence forever.

High Mass

Winter Sundays,
when my father was on strike from steel,
he and my mother woke late,
then rose and prepared for high mass
at Saints Peter and Paul.

Wandering into their room,
I climbed into the four-poster cherry bed
they bought at May Stern
the month before marrying in 1947—
warm from their bodies, their scent,
its voluminous spread
and blankets enveloping me.

My mother in a slip, at her vanity,
watched me watch her in its mirror.
Eyebrows arched, mouth slightly open,
tongue dabbing at her upper lip—
the way women unconsciously arrange
their faces when making-up—
she plucked and painted, brushed
forever her long brown hair,
circled her mouth with a golden tube of lipstick,
and pressed her red lips together in a kiss.
Around her neck fastened pearls,
dipped each ear to earring,
slipped into her dress and called,
Joe, my father's name, to zip it.

Dark, clean-shaven,
he stood at the bureau—
where they kept insurance policies,
immunization records,
secret envelopes—
choosing a necktie and handkerchief.
His white shirt had French cuffs, ruby cufflinks.
He smiled at me.
That quickly he had her fastened,
his red silk tie looped,
without even looking
into a perfect four-in-hand.

My mother, a seamstress, inspected him,
then patted his blue suit lapel.
She made my sister's clothes.
Those mornings, my father in the house,
we weren't rushed and resigned.
We ate eggs and bacon
and rode to church in the Plymouth.
Marie and I learned as children
never to cross a picket line.

Holy God

Suspended stories above the nave,
Saints Peter and Paul's Gothic choir loft
took one thousand trees to carve.
Its sad rose window
stared at Larimer Avenue.
Mammoth zinc organ pipes fluted the walls.

Marooned in our Italian parish,
Miss Claire, the blonde Irish organist,
spun pale hands across the keys,
pumped the pedals,
closed her blue eyes and signaled
the dire prelude to "Holy God."
The choir loft heaved,
heavy with the organ's engine.

Six years old, robed and surpliced,
clutching a Gregorian Missal,
I took my cues from her mouth,
as if mine on hers—
the first time I hallucinated in church:
Jesus stirred on His altar cross,
releasing me from my body; and I realized,
as I floated over the congregation,
how poorly words serve longing.

It was the Feast of the Epiphany, 1959.
My father was on strike from the steel mill.
I peered down, and there he was,
pushing along the pews
a long-handled reed alms basket,
working his way through the north
and south transepts, then the nave,
row upon row, down the long stone aisle,
until the narthex where the ushers gathered,
after Offertory to count the money.

Sun stole through the stained glass,
superimposing in a blast of bloody light
the Communion of Saints on the chancel walls;
and, for an instant, I was blinded.
Then I was back in the loft
with the other choir boys,
waiting for Miss Claire's eyes to open—
that look of ecstasy she flashed me—
before they closed again
and she began to sing.

The Cold War

Fourth grade, the year I had Miss Manso,
the pretty lay teacher,
I sat next to the window
and watched dogs mate on Flavel Street.

Miss Manso lived on Apple Avenue.
She neither beat nor insulted me.
In secret I loved her.
She could have been a movie star like Patricia Neal

in *The Day the Earth Stood Still.*
Men like Michael Rennie rented rooms in our neighborhood.
The psychic Jeane Dixon predicted children
would be kidnapped by angels;

there were passages in Saint John's *Apocalypse*
describing our assumption:
Then I saw heaven opened,
and there was a white horse!

I prayed to be spirited off by the firmament,
far from the furnace of nuns.
A space race was on.
Castro was a monster.

In Cuba swam a Bay of Pigs.
Khrushchev vowed to bury us. Idolators,
we worshipped Kennedy.
Those dogs on Flavel Street knew what was coming:

woozy gaits, maudlin sidelong glances.
Like drunkards, they were the dogs of drunkards.
Their keening prelude heralded,
then subsumed, the air-raid siren—

stupid heads thrown back as they yowled.
We'd finally been called to answer.
The Russians were coming to collect.
This time it was real.

We rose by rote from our desks,
and placed perpendicular to our lips,
as we'd been taught, index fingers
vowing us to silence—

no matter what might happen.
We'd seen the pictures.
We knew about Radio Free Europe.
At the snap of Miss Manso's fingers,

I linked hands with my partner, Tommy Cervone,
and followed her from the room,
behind marching queues of the other seven grades,
led by black-shrouded nuns,

snowy bibs like sickles sliced across their breasts.
Down past Our Lady's alcove,
where she mooned placid, blue and beautiful—
almost drugged, flashing back

(The Annunciation had blown her mind)—
between the milk machine and janitor's snow plow.
To the school basement bomb shelter,
the condemned haunted bowling alley.

Beneath long lunch tables we crouched,
fingers stitched to our lips,
siren and curs wailing,
the nuns unstrapping colossal rosaries

from their hips—like *West Side Story*—
readying for the siege, chanting
Hail Marys. Druidic. The elite.
In their martyrdom, they'd take down minions.

We were to pray silently for the Communists,
our separated brethren.
That's how we would save ourselves—
by bartering with God

for a niche in the hereafter.
The explosion would kill everyone.
I looked out from under my table;
all I could see was Miss Manso's skirt.

Black, it fell just below her knees.
Her legs so white. She wore black
orthopaedic shoes. Deformed.
I knew I'd never marry her.

The Communists had hold of her mind.
They demanded she denounce God.
On the cellar crucifix suffered the Christ
who had foretold to the syllable the 20th century.

I felt so sorry for Him:
the crosshairs of zero hour,
thief in the night. Such brilliance.
The darkening schoolyard whispered His name.

He looked straight at me,
and I knew it was okay.
He'd been playing possum all along.
I disengaged my hand from Tommy's.

His eyes were closed. He held his breath,
praying like a little priest, fist against his chest,
giving himself Extreme Unction.
Perhaps the bomb had dropped.

The 13th Sunday after Pentecost

There it loomed,
when I burst through the front door—
calamitous newsreel glyphs
across the flushed brow
of the big boxy black-and-white TV:
Abortion and the Law,
a CBS News Special Report.
In the ashtray, my dad's Camel smoldered,
mother's thimble and pinking shears,
the *TV Guide,* in her lap.
When I asked what *abortion* meant,
they shot each other panicked looks.
A blood-red *69*
I thought was just a number
splashed my football jersey.

The next day was Labor Day,
the day after that my first day
of 5th grade at Saints Peter and Paul
with Sister Mercedes and her fraternity paddle,
dime-sized holes drilled through its teak face,
rawhide thong to wrap her wrist.
Three days earlier, Martin Luther King
had stood before the Lincoln Memorial:
"1963 is not an end, but a beginning."
Bewitched by Vatican II,
at our throats dangled chained medallions
of the skull-capped pontiff,
John XXIII, in relief.
Buddhist monks doused themselves in gasoline,
then rocked in immolation.

Behind our alley duplex,
oracle fire roared from 55 gallon salamanders.
In a span of abandoned insulbrick shacks,
swooning from The Hollow cliffs,
derelict angels slept in shattered glass and newsprint.
Motorcycles revved. Girls got in trouble.
The Kingsmen's "Louie Louie" was the year's biggest hit.
My friends and I—
mother called them my *boyfriends*—
played it incessantly on the high-fidelity.
The FBI investigated its coded lyrics.
Everything would be subtracted from us.
The truth mattered less every day.
At the end of that year, our house,
by order of eminent domain, was demolished.
Saints Peter and Paul sealed its red school doors forever.

I smoked cigarettes and set fires,
studied stolen pictures of naked women,
dreamt of being loved forever.
The Dodgers beat the Yankees
four straight in the World Series.
JFK's motorcade threaded by
the Texas School Book Depository.
Jackie's pink suit and pillbox.
15,000 military advisers in Vietnam.
Patrick Henry in the school play,
I memorized his entire speech of 1775
to the Virginia Convention
at Saint John's Church in Richmond.

I never should've asked my mother and father
such a question—about abortion:
the way they stared at each other
across the living room, as if they'd just met,
as if I'd spied them at something dirty.
They never answered.
I kissed them goodnight, then up to my bedroom.
They called *Good night, sleep tight,*
don't let the bed bugs bite.
It was the 13th Sunday after Pentecost.
I know this from The Table of Movable Feasts
in the *Saint Joseph's Sunday Missal* I kept nearby.
In jagged penmanship Sister whipped me for,
I had entered, with my first fountain pen,
in the flyleaf, the date of its receipt:
July 20, 1963—my 10th birthday.
Six years, to the day, a man stood on the moon.
Give me liberty or give me death.

Sister Thomasine

In Catechism, Sister Thomasine taught
that we had fashioned Christ's cross
in our venial little forges.
Hundred-handed, we were the original
monstrous forms, banished from Earth
by the Gods—no better than Pagans.
We were *broomsticks, washerwomen.*
Look what you have done to Him,
she gabbled. *Look:* pointing,
up at the crucifix—Jesus famished
for privacy—her blowfish white wrist,
the nubbed fingerette—a birth defect—
no nail, not even skin, just bone
at its glaring tip discharged
from her voluminous black sleeve.
You may say fuck, she liked to remind us,
but dasn't say Jesus.
She loathed the girls—*bold as brass*—
the pretty little frills she'd never had.
She would have murdered them,
the *floozies.* They tinkled and wept.
Face like a catcher's mitt;
Leviathan breasts, Tweedledee
and Tweedledum, woozy
as a couple of Flavel Street drunks.
She boxed the boys' ears in the cloak room,
dangling the tiniest from hat racks,
chanting in spectral metrics,
like the chorus in *Medea,*
"Little Red Caboose."
Even in His anguish,
Jesus remained composed,
winningly handsome,
trying not to laugh.

Good Friday: March 24, 1967

Here since noon we've languished—
platoon of voyeurs,
dug in for the death watch.
Spread in the pew before me are 8th-grade girls:
pleated plaid jumpers, chaste milky blouses,
black lace mantillas falling
over long Irish yellow hair—
so desirable the temple curtain at 3 sharp
rends in twain and Jesus, as we witness,
expires from sheer boredom.
Poor Jesus. I have always loved Him:
His carpenter's apron, ball-peen,
mouthful of twelve-pennies,
square, rule, awl and plane.
That rank of girls, however,
ripe sheaves forbidden, deranges me.
In my grief, I smirk with lust,
envisioning them, God forgive me,
unclothed. Lightning flashes.
Thunder, then diluvium. On cue,
I make the Sign of the Cross
with my classmates, and nearly faint
from Sister Fatima's jumbo rosary
raked across my back.
Telegnostic bride of Christ,
she's decoded my impure thoughts.
By an ear I'm towed to the Tabernacle,
hurled to the stone floor, made to kneel
at the foot of the cross upon my hands.
The pain is instant, then expands:
the fathomless mystery of infinity.
A brilliant tactic designed not merely
to break me, but assure me
what will follow is unimaginable.

Catacombs, crawling with Communists,
snake beneath the nave and transepts—
as was all along foretold:
Viet Cong with rusty spikes,
sledges with nine-pound heads to hammer them,
crosses for each of us.

Emerson Street

This is the exact spot
on Emerson Street
where August Dolan kicked me
so spectacularly in the balls,
that I dropped to my knees, whispered *Oh*
and coughed out a baby blackbird—
the aftermath of my innocence—
that flew off and took its place
in the sycamores with the other crows
gathered to witness my revenge.
Augie twisted out of his coat,
but I grabbed his tie,
garroting him one-handed,
sizing up his reddening face with my free fist.
Even now I feel with pleasure his chubby
cheek blacken on my knuckles.
Sister Aloysius Gonzaga,
Sacred Heart's simian principal—
she favored Zira, the hazel-eyed
chimpanzee animal psychologist,
played by Kim Hunter
in *Planet of the Apes*—
witnessed the entire affair
from her office, hauled us in,
back-handed Augie so hard,
his scorched face peeled by lunch,
knocked us both into the marble stairwell
with a titanium yardstick, then whaled
the Communion of Saints out of us as we lay there—
prompting the life-size statue
of Our Lady of Perpetual Help
to jitter on her plinth,

though she winked
when I gazed up at her in my stupor.
Birds have testicles,
but keep them hidden
inside their bodies.

Brooks Brothers Shirts

Ten hours a day,
my mother hunched downtown
in Brooks Brothers tailor shop—fretting
cuffs and belt loops, pleats, vents,

buttonholes, lapels into ruthless
wool suits, unthinkably expensive,
for men who spent their days unsoiled,
whose soft hands never raised a callous.

After she punched out,
caught the streetcar, and high-heeled home
two icy downhill blocks
from the Callowhill stop,

she often breezed in with packages:
icy broadcloth shirts she'd monogrammed
with my initials,
swathed in smoky silvery tissue.

The deep navy boxes piped in gold,
the gold band that bound them,
and in their centers
the Brooks Brothers coat of arms:

a golden ewe lowered on a sling
into a sacrificial grail.
The "Agnus Dei."
My mother dressed me like a prince.

"Apparel doth proclaim the man,"
I'd one day read in *Hamlet.*
Those luscious shirts:
the forbidden glory of plenty

(of too much, really),
they privileged me
among my parents' oppressors.
Every day with neckties, blazers,

oxblood penny loafers, Princeton wave
that swooped my yearning brow,
I wore them to school: blue, pink, yellow,
charcoal and burgundy pin-stripe, tattersall,

blinding ecclesiastical white.
I wore them to church.
I adored those shirts,
my immaculate patrician destiny.

My mother washed them by hand,
hung to dry in the winter sun,
spritzed with water from an Iron City pony,
then shelved them in plastic bags

overnight in the freezer.
She loved them as much as I did.
My father, a steelworker, a crane-climber—
he loved them too.

He didn't want me to get my hands dirty.
He wanted me to work for myself.
My mother ironed in the cellar
where my father shaved

out of an enamel basin with hot water
from the washtub, a small mirror
on a nail pounded into the block wall
he whitewashed every year.

On his work bench she stationed
a sleeve board for the long tedium
of the crease, true as a plumb line,
dabs of starch at collar and cuff,

shots of steam from the iron's black button,
mother's needle hand steering
the hissing wedge just shy of scorching
the frozen fabric (which is the charm).

My shirts were sharp enough to bring blood.
Monday through Friday, school,
then Sunday, High Mass,
the shirts awaited me, dangling on hangers

from the cellar's copper ceiling pipes,
six of them in a skirmish,
nudging one another in the darkness,
complicit in my certain future,

swaying slightly, like a slow dance,
in the heat vent's tepid whisper—
at their throats the oval writ:
Brooks Brothers Makers Est 1818.

The Pittsburgh Athletic Association

Braced at its threshold—built in homage
to a Venetian Renaissance Palace—
was a mammoth coin of Mercury,
the soul's escort to the underworld.
Wings sprouted from his hard hat.
Chiseled beneath the bronze profile—
scarred nose and brow,
insolent jaw of a *fabbro*
blacksmith from Puglia—
were Roman numerals: MCMVIII.

The lobby walls were paneled oak;
ceilings inlaid with shields;
floral maudlin carpet;
golden elevators; andirons,
gaudy as Processional crosses;
and, above the fireplace, a gigantic oil:
naked men bathing in smoky columned pools,
a turbaned Moor in vestments
on his knees to towel a bather.

The day I slipped in with David Friday,
as his father's guest,
I was thirteen years old, no legacy,
no obvious future—but a Latin name
flourished with vowels.
My dad was a millwright,
son of a *fabbro* from Puglia.

In the antique gym, old men lobbed
medicine balls, limbered at the pommel horse,
chinning bar and dumbbells.
A punch-drunk heavy bag swayed.
Knotted sea ropes dangled from rafters.
The swimming pool spangled with sun from the skylight.
The locker room was carpeted, lockers rattan.
Cigarettes and aftershave, burbling whirlpools.
Squash players, twirling rackets,
strolled naked to the showers and rubbing tables,
mounted the half-ton porcelain scale,
registering their worth to the decimal.

We dropped our towels for the porter to retrieve.
He wore an ice cream coat
and ran a whisk broom over us
as we hurried to lunch:
Welsh Rarebit on toast points,
Cokes over ice.
In dark lounges colluded billiard balls.
Pins screamed from the bowling alley.
David signed for everything.

Connecticut

The unfathomable speed the jet achieved
as it screeched off the macadam
was what I burned for that last summer
in '67 before I entered high school.
My first plane ride, my first trek
out of Pittsburgh, to visit family
in Danbury, I sat buckled on the wing
next to my mother and sister.

An inch away, through the square pane,
lay eternity, a vague marbling blue
and white vapor. As we dropped
beneath the clouds, earth appeared:
green tilled fields—so lusciously limned,
I soared like an addict
in New England's burnished ether.
My song was "The Letter," by the Boxtops.
Perhaps *my baby* was under one
of those Thoreauvian thatches,
inking my name to the crest
of her monogrammed stationary.
That entire week in Connecticut, I searched for her.
But the only women I glimpsed
were those I'd traveled with, and Aunt Pat
and her three baby daughters, too terrified
to toddle into a room were I in it—
as if my garish longing
sutured along my forehead.

There was a hoop in the driveway,
but only a volleyball to shoot with.
Uncle John, an engineer, came home late every day.
He didn't know what to do with me.
Dark hair sprouted from my pores,
under my arms. After dinner,
he drove us through his immaculate suburb,
then to Maple Hill for ice cream.
Marriage seemed effortless:
biding cheer and civility,
the odd acquisitive bent toward children.

Days, I lay sweating at the club pool
in new too-tight gold bathing trunks
my mother insisted I have for the trip.
My sister, with Victorian self-possession,
processed through Austen and Eliot,
while I read a story in *Ladies Home Journal*—
sentence by sentence, the same sentence—
about a woman alone, behind a locked door,
bathwater gushing into the long white tub,
her unclothed body at its secret office.

Stag

The lights are doused.
Eight millimeter black and white
chops through the rented projector
onto a bedsheet fastened
with steak knives to the wall.
No sound, save the panting sprockets,
beers *shissing* open, struck matches,
the steady aspiration of the groom and his ushers.

In her bath robe, a housewife, haggard,
lank-haired, holds a flashlight
for the tongue-tied electrician,
ill-at-ease in his work-fatigues,
fat kind face, Carmine
scripted on his breast pocket.
Breakfast still not tidied,
a tribunal of immaculate appliances—
coffee percolator, waffle iron and mixer,
the discreet toaster—remains mute
on the counter. No longer
can she hold in her hunger,
evident in her famished eyes.
But there is also dread to her desire—
the way she stabs the cigarette into her mouth—
as if she has but a short time to live
a life that has been brute and cut-rate,
something pathetically beautiful in the tepid shaft
she sprays in the morning kitchen darkness
on the fuse box that Carmine tinkers with:
a half-exposed truth aching
for a sliver more illumination.
Baby angels float through its smoky light.

Then everyone laughs,
and the man and woman, as if on cue,
hurl themselves at each other,
shedding clothes as if out of fire,
their flesh like undressed baby dolls,
neutered in the antique celluloid:
Carmine—thick, hairy; the woman—
discreet pubis, flat-chested.
His dark digs into her pale.
The kisses. Like a grainy scandal sheet candid:
the withering absence of privacy.
They speed through their lust
in Gatling fits, like Chaplin going at it;
then excruciating slow motion
and zooms inside their bodies.
Out of her mouth spill silent words
into the mouth of the man on the linoleum,
words inured to the likes of us, forbidden,
intimate. She cries out;
that's what she must be doing.
He pets her, whispers her name
with his carnal Sicilian lips—
whatever her name might be.
This could be love.

Noosed from its doorknob,
the matrimonial tux—
silky lapels, cummerbund,
pleated alabaster shirt—
witnesses every bit of it.
For now there's just the paroxysm
of machinery. The film beam
gags on cigarette smoke.

The North Game

Dulce et decorum est pro patria mori
—Horace, by way of Wilfred Owen's "Dulce et Decorum Est"

The statue of Our Lady of Victory
presides in the Quadrangle
like a warhead on its launch pad.
Through a portal secreted in ivy,
we enter the Christian Brothers hermitage,
wind the vault down into its medieval chapel:
ruby ether, smoking icons,
reek of myrrh and niter.
On the altar lambrequin
are a solid gold cross, like a Roman short sword;
chalice, pall and purificator,
chalice veil; ciborium, paten;
cruets of amber Tokay.

At Coach Wheeler's command,
we forty-four kneel. In white vestments,
symbolizing innocence and triumph,
Father Pilarski, a Navy priest, says Mass—
though it seems a ruse, this season of Requiem.
At Fort Benning, Calley's on trial for My Lai.
Father prays God we win, in expiation
of our sins, that we come away whole
in person and faith. United
in that desire, we step to the rail,
take upon our tongues the Eucharist;
then file, silent, through the narthex
where the bronze tablet lists its roll
of *Faithfully Departed:* boys
from world wars I and II, Korea,
and now the inaugural dead
of our war, Vietnam.

We chant vespers, dirge out the Alma Mater—
Under your Towers moves life's eternal May—
as we march down the ramp to the bus,
toting sea bags: helmets, spikes, pads,
blue and gold game jerseys—
the commingled remains of all that's been forgotten.
We've no idea what we'll walk into once we cross
the colossal bridge over the Allegheny—
where plenty of kids lose heart; others, their minds;
even their eternal souls—to play the Trojans,
those animals from the North Side.

Those of us who return:
our parents and girls will be waiting
in the school cafeteria.
They'll rise and applaud as we stagger in.
On its run along the river, a freighter howls.
Endless mills mass black and smoldering,
forging ample steel to convene the Apocalypse.
The clocks have been turned back:
five o'clock. It's pitch black.

The Lobotomy Running Schenley Oval

He runs winters shod in ice,
a vest of snow salting his bare chest,
wind throttling Old Glory
on its Panther Hollow flagpole;
summers, bleeding sweat
along the scorched asphalt,
sun braced atop his half-shaven head:
one hemisphere for the shag to his shoulders;
the other, egg-slick, branded
with the silver omega-shaped scar
leavened on his frontal bone.
Revolution upon revolution,
as if circling Schenley Oval—
where the young queue in cars,
deflowering 1969—
is a sentence adjudicated by the gods
for some mythic impropriety.
For all time—love
scalped from his memory,
vacant eyes trained perpetually ahead—
he spins on the armature of his own curse.
Even as night pours out
its darkness, he appears—
parked lovers emerging
from swoons along the Oval curb,
engaging their headlights—
a shadow darting
among the chaste sycamores.

Migraine

There is a mechanism,
perhaps secreted in the clitoris,
or even deeper, in the glint
of a blue eye registering fear
and desire commingled like blood
and milk that triggers migraine
in the throes of orgasm.

She will say four days later—
when the attack slackens
and she can brook speech,
after the flicker from a match head
and the killdeer crying no longer convulse her—
that it lit upon her like an angel
washed in blood—
Joan of Arc, ablaze
at the foot of the bed, beckoning.

Months can go by without one.
She forgets the pain,
like an amnesiac her name,
until the smell of overripe peaches,
a naked man asking, gently, "Shall I go on?"
and her own voice, Lethean,
an octave from screaming,
the correct response eluding her.
Whether it is "No, don't stop"
or "Yes, don't stop."
No and *Yes* in tiny detonations.

Eyes rucked shut, she tries to pry away
the pinions attached to her temples.
Through gossamer eyelids
blue light bores the ceiling.
Off the sheet she levitates,
breasts like the shocked faces of newborns,
her soft belly, white
columns of her legs, dangling feet,
the black veil of long falling hair.

III. Genitori

Everything
they do is wrong, and the worst thing,
they all do it, is to die.
—WILLIAM MEREDITH, "PARENTS"

Angels

In the hospital waiting room,
you catch a TV highlight
of a Grapefruit League game.
Randy Johnson, like a tetched kestrel-
faced prophet, lurches
off the mound with a fastball.
Across the strike zone swoops a dove,
maybe an angel. You're in Pittsburgh,
March; it's snowing. All week
you've seen angels; everyone's tired,
proclaiming even horrid things angels,
intimating miracles. Johnson's pitch
obliterates the bird—
a hail of feathers and dander,
as if inside a tiny bomb detonated.
Like a cartoon. Thoroughly unbelievable.
Around you, people are dying.
But you ignore it.
You laugh at the massacred dove.
It's not funny, but you laugh.
You could cry, rip your hair out, your clothes off,
crash through the seventh-floor window
into the slushy black streets of the city.
It's funny because it's not.
The clip plays over and over,
eight, nine times in slower and slower motion:
the windup, the pitch, then the bird
blows off the screen like smoke.
Each time you laugh. Hard.
The way as a kid in school,
when a nun was beating the living
angels out of you with her fists,
and you wanted to kill her, you'd laugh
and laugh and laugh.

The Little Noise

A rhythmic sough escapes the bathroom
where my mother showers.
Too much pressure on the tap,
the ancient plumbing convulses;
air, the culprit, trapped in the stream.

I pause outside the bathroom,
listen, then silently turn the knob
and peer into the steam.
Behind the marbled glass
shower door, her back's to me,
bent body white as a clock face,
shower cap mushroomed on her head.
Astonished to still be alive
after all these years, she is the one—
making the little noise,
mewling like a lost violin,
scrabbling with a washcloth one-handed
to scrub herself, the last dignity;
clutching with the other the steel bar
my father riveted in the tile wall to steady her.

I close the door,
pad across the hall, sit on her bed,
silver cane racked over the stead,
medicine bottles deployed and numbered
on her dresser doilies.
There are nights when she can't undo the lids;
she starts to sweat, when all the give in her
relaxes and she leaks that noise,
the sound of love—
hate is a different noise—
but a love that shakes her
like a vile parent shakes a child
and she begins to cry.
My father and I finally get her to bed.
I say good night, walk the long hall
out of their apartment building,
behind each forgetful door
the conspiratorial murmur of TVs.

At vigil, my father sits in the living room.
All night he listens for my mother,
as one listens for a bedded baby,
straining to reckon that sound,
the little noise he's heard before,
but can't recall
until his head drops to his chest,
flesh-colored hearing aids
like fetuses curled in his ears.

My Mother and Father Falling

The cereal box is anathema,
too far back in the cabinet
for my arthritic mother to reach.
She'd rather topple from the stool
she drags over to climb than accept
the gnarled hand my father proffers.

Her fall is inevitable. Straight back
like a ponderous fish flailing for its bed of bones,
my father there to net her in his gray arms
gone to slag; the two of them,
husband and wife, annealed to each other
in the sacrament of Matrimony,
swooning into the ether, before whatever soured.

Fifty-eight years they've perfected this ritual,
again and again, like high-wire mates:
she falling, he catching.
Yet today what's ahead dissolves:
cable severed, transformer blown.
Lamps flicker, then snuff.
The hissing kettle sputters and expires.

Out of the kitchen they walk,
through the dark silent apartment,
down the long ivory corridor,
pass through the glass front doors
and catch the streetcar to the end of the line:
laving years off their long sentences,
before any of us, before anything.

Joe and Rose

This year my mother insists
my dad not break ground.
She doesn't want him out of her sight.
All he needs to do is fall.
She asks if I notice a difference.
He's thin, holds his coffee in two hands.
No garden this year. But he doesn't listen.
He rents a patch along the golf course—
Too big. What's he trying to prove?—
and goes about it the same as always:
seeds and plants, manure and fertilizer,
in good conscience, and sacramental care.
He drives up the slope,
his long-handled spade, hoe and rake
tied in the trunk. Across the fairway,
he drags the hose, spirits home
to my little boys the golf balls
he finds. A dozen kinds of lettuce,
thirty tomato plants. Peppers. Eggplant.
Delivers it all to my mother.
She doesn't know what to do with it.
My God, Joe. There's just the two of us.
She brags about his garden:
how at 90 he can outwork any kid,
how hard his head is.

Haircut

Bagnio Vicas's barbershop
wedged the nexus of Omega Street,
Hoeveler Bridge, and Hamilton Avenue,
its ceremonial striped helix
of whirling red, white, and blue,
like prelude to a dream.

Bagnio in broken English
admonished me to "Sit still"
on the booster lanced across the porcelain
arms of the chrome chair he jacked
with his lever, swiveled on a whim,
revved silver clippers boiling
at my nape, dun strop,
heavy-hanging, cadaverous,
upon which he scourged
his pearl-handled straight razor.

He'd slice my throat if I didn't mind—
the way he spun my head in his gorgeous
hands, manicured cuticles,
nails precisely filed, fey
as the Pope's Pontifical purple gloves;
blinding white belted *tunica;*
the disintegration of his Lucky Strike,
an inch from my eye, in his smoking lips,
the white scar bisecting them—
reminder of the One True Cross.

Bagnio, Calabrian Cary Grant,
nightshade lethal—
though *fairy,* some whispered.
He seemed nothing like a fairy—
more Captain Hook,
with his choir of asses.
My mother loathed him: *gavone,*
gangster-pretty, boot-black razor-cut.
She had his number—
his beautiful wife was a tramp—
even if he did sing angelically *La Bohème*
as he pecked at my ears, slant smile
that necromanced Divine Providence
postulants strolling past his shop to the convent.
The hot lather cruet burbled Godlessly.
He owned the torch and candles, salves
and unguents. Negroes came to him
for fire cuts, processes—in confidence,
secret as a laboratory.
Tonsorial stench.
Labyrinthine mirrors.
Hair sprouted from his floor.
In the back room, with the brooms,
lounged pornography.

I coveted the pink casket of Bazooka
he rewarded me with,
the sugar-powdered shrunken comic
pressed in with it: Bazooka Joe
and his Magic Circle Club.
I sent away for the decoder ring.
I swore an oath.
My father, on the elevated shine stand,
kept vigil. He knew
I hated Bagnio's black scissors,
its blind rat-tail eye, flying at me
like Hitchcock's grackles.

He held my hand
as we crossed Hamilton
to the listing Spignos Club
for rigatoni, and Tom Tucker pop—
the legend, *Spignos Saturnia,*
chiseled into the Tuscan tile
crowning the flatiron:
Carrara marble and blond brick.
It threatened to plunge off the bridge
into the Hollow. With his pocket knife,
he diced pears into his Chianti,
and fed them to me on a spoon.
He wouldn't die for a half a century,
but I missed him already.

My Father at the Montréal Musée des Beaux-Arts

I stroll into an alcove
and there on a blunt onyx plinth
sits my father, cross-legged, dozing,

perfectly rendered
in prefigurement hundreds of years ago.
The modesty of the piece is typical of him,

titled simply by the curators,
or even the archaeologist
who catalogued it at the excavation site:

Seated Old Man. Described:
"Buff pottery with traces of pigment,
Late classic Vera Cruz 600–1000."

He wears the ceremonial cap, scars
along the outsized ochre hands knotted
in his lap. Earrings trumpet

out of majestic ears. The long scimitar
of the nose, lower lip reposed.
Like coming upon his final reverie

in the kitchen on Mellon Street,
after he has eased from the bottom
rung of the boom crane

he's been fastened to for millennia.
Punched out, shirtless, the hair on his chest
wintry, the kitchen, with its whispering

white icebox, preternaturally hushed,
light scrolling over it, shot and beer
before him like decanted amber—

an appeasement to the unappeasable God
of Steel. My father: alone
in the gallery of his mythic past—

he has forded rivers
of forgetfulness—where no one
save I may trespass.

Bracciole

With the cast-iron claw
hammer—burnished
silver in endless
bouts of fire, forged
in Manfredonia, Puglia,
by my blacksmith
grandfather, Paolo
Battiante, arrived
on the *Luisiana,*
out of the province of Foggia,
1907, Ellis Island,
where his name was altered,
like so many, the hammer
secreted in his tunic—
my mother pounds
on butcher block
flank steak to temper,
then layers each pliant tongue
with olive oil, garlic, parsley,
salt and pepper, before
trussing them into scrolls
bound with string
from Stagno's Bakery,
and dropping them
into the incarnadine
majesty of the sauce to roil
the rest of our lives. Amen.

The Hour of the Wolf

(after the film by Ingmar Bergman)

Out in the halls it is 1953.
Cigarettes are innocent as babies.
My father wanders
smoking one after another.
He is pure narrative,
reliable as plot;
but, outside the frame,
he can only imagine
what birth might be *like.*

Too late for prep and saddle block,
my mother is rushed into delivery,
a stanzaic space of white
hush and glisten.
We've rehearsed this from memory,
this way of getting here
because there is no other way—
wholly derivative,
a throwback to ancient form:
diction, syntax, the spondaic
utterance that signals the pang
of common language.

A floor-length mirror
is placed at my mother's feet;
and there—sentient, ignorant,
shunted into worlds of narcissism
and silence—we meet.

The First Sunday of Advent

Traveling south out of Pittsburgh—
this recessional day of buck season,
as if impaling the earth—we plummet
into West Virginia.
Its stars, omnisciently white, auger
like drill bits through steel-gray clouds
atop the car, and read our minds.
November, in troubled sleep, cries out
in winter bodement, unleashes its snow,
slips into drugged solstice.

The cast of light—slant,
seductive, mannered as Pasolini,
an impending light—passes over us its wand.
Strapped fitfully behind Joan and me
our babies murmur prophetically.
We play See 'n' Say.
What does the cow say?
Joan pulls the string:
a long, long *moo* we all as one *moo.*
What does the duck say? We *quack.*
The pig ? Oink. We read
The Teddy Bears' Picnic:
"*If you go down*
In in the woods today
You'd better not go alone
It's lovely down in the woods today
But safer to stay home."

Nude trees, embittered by thwarted lives
to coal rooted, gnarl.
Shoulders frock with corpses:
balletic hooves mid-kick arrested,
cracked eyes, swirling racks.
Summits brace with Coffindaffer crosses.
Owls in daylight—an Appalachian omen—
preside the transverse beams.
Occasional shades, like breath configuring
on a pane, take shape among the snowy trees.

We hurtle past the Puritan house in Jane Lew:
immured ancient brick, candles guttering
in curtained yearning gables.
The road whitens, black consent
in the veins mined beneath us.
In its gorge tumults the New.
Pterodactyls lift and circle.

Burying Saint Joseph

When, after forty-two months,
the farm house we left behind
in Statesville has not sold,
I finally heed mother's directive
to bury in the yard
a statue of Saint Joseph.
He will effect what no realtor
has the savvy for.
My mother presents this as dogma:
the same causal inevitability
as landing a little place in Heaven
through rosaries and Novenas.
Along the pump house,
above which hover impatiens
and demure Lily of the valley,
I drive a spade, drop to my knees
with my old friend, St. Joe,
won in a third grade spelling bee:
two inches of phosphorescent plastic
that gleamed miraculously in the dark
of my first bedroom on Prince Street.
He's traveled house to house,
into my manhood and marriage,
his wry smile effaced over the years,
in his right arm clutched his baby boy,
the unsuspecting Christ, like a sack
of 3-penny finishing nails.
As instructed, I inter him head down,
in the fashion of Peter's crucifixion,
face him east, to assume the sun
by day; all night, the moon.

He ignites the subterranean quartz
and hiddenite. Pooled above him,
on the parched earth surface,
glows a crown of milky light.
Black Widow spiderlings
flash their scarlet fetish,
and scatter in the rosemary.
The house sells in a fortnight.

Labriola's

Entering, through the medium
of *memoria,* achieves the parable

of Proust: the aroma
of *Italianata,* opera of olfactory,

blood-gnosis spinning me back
over these scored plank floors

grouted with *appassionata*
to Sundays after Mass fifty years ago,

when Larimer Avenue was *Paradiso*
and my parents held the hands

of my sister and me as we processed
along Labriola's aisles

of *melanzano, romas,* Fiorella
pears, pews of garlic, *basilico.*

Litany of olives:
green, black, cracked,

Siciliano, Milanese,
Calabrese. Salami,

sopprassata, mortadella,
wheels of *formaggio* from Palermo,

Abruzzi, Formicolo.
Lexicon of *Mangiare.*

Bread of each province.
Theology of pasta:

spool, labyrinth, conundrum,
geometry—vowels falling

like *pastina* from the rafters
where a scratchy Vivaldi sonata

wafts like DeNobili smoke.
Among the promenade of shades,

trembling a spectral *tarantella,*
market the ghosts of my mother

and father, shawl and fedora—
Domenico Giuseppe, Maria Rosalina—

heads bowed at the sacred occasion
of the larder,

fingers scribbling deliriously
in the clouds of plentitude.

Acknowledgments

Grateful acknowledgment is extended to the following journals in which some of these poems, in some cases different versions, first appeared:

"Burying Saint Joseph": *Adanna;* "The Thirteenth Sunday after Pentecost": *Asheville Poetry Review;* "Baseball": *Aethlon: The Journal of Sport Literature;* "Bracciole": *Alimentum;* "My Father at the Montréal Musée des Beaux-Arts": *The Cincinnati Review;* "The Little Noise," "Migraine," and "My Mother and Father Falling": *Connotation Press: An Online Artifact;* "Sister Thomasine": *Ecotone;* "Pass Over My Life in Silence": *88: A Journal of Contemporary Poetry;* "Angels" and "Sleepwalking in Purgatory": *Explorations: The 20th Century;* "Labriola's": *Italian Americana;* "Affliction" and "The Huckster": *The Louisville Review;* "The Hour of the Wolf": *North Carolina Humanities;* "Good Friday: March 24, 1967": *Poet Lore;* "Emerson Street," "Haircut," and "The North Game": *Prairie Schooner;* "Brooks Brothers Shirts": *The Progressive;* "The Lobotomy Running Schenley Oval": *Puerto del Sol;* "Joe and Rose: *VIA: Voices in Italian Americana;* "The Cold War": *War, Literature & Arts.*

"DiDomeni" was the winner of the 2014 Rita Dove Prize, awarded annually by the Center for Women Writers at Salem College.

FIV

CPSIA information can be obtained
at www.ICGtesting.com
Printed in the USA
LVOW12s1442011016
507007LV00001B/168/P

1/17